Dances Learned Last Night

Michael Donaghy was born in the Bronx, New York, in 1954. His collections to date are *Shibboleth* (1988), which won the Whitbread Prize for Poetry and the Geoffrey Faber Memorial Prize, *Errata* (1993), which received awards from the Arts Council of England and the Ingram Merrill Foundation, and *Conjure* (2000). In 1985 he moved to London, where he works as a teacher and musician.

Also by Michael Donaghy

Conjure

MICHAEL DONAGHY

Dances Learned Last Night

Poems 1975–1995

PICADOR

First published 2000 by Picador
an imprint of Macmillan Publishers Ltd
25 Eccleston Place, London SW1W 9NF
Basingstoke and Oxford
Associated companies throughout the world
www.macmillan.com

Shibboleth originally published 1988 by Oxford University Press,
including 'Slivers' and 'Reader' and a different version of 'Letter'.
Errata originally published 1993 by Oxford University Press.

ISBN 0 330 48194 0

1 3 5 7 9 8 6 4 2

A CIP catalogue record for this book is available from
the British Library.

Typeset by SetSystems Ltd, Saffron Walden, Essex
Printed and bound in Great Britain by
Mackays of Chatham plc, Chatham, Kent

Contents

Acknowledgements – ix

SHIBBOLETH

Machines – 3

Pentecost – 4

A Miracle – 5

Analysand – 6

More Machines – 8

Deceit – 9

The Present – 10

Touch – 11

Music and Sex and Drinking – 12

'Smith' – 13

Cadenza – 15

Letter – 17

Shibboleth – 19

Quorum – 20

Auto da Fé – 21

Ramon Fernandez? – 22

Partisans – 23

Majority – 24

News Item – 25

Pornography – 26

Footage from the Interior – 27

Khalypso – 29

The Bacchae – 30

A Disaster – 31

Starlet – 32

Interviews – 33

Remembering Steps to Dances Learned Last Night – 36

The Tuning – 38

Rational Construction – 39

The Dreamer and the Dreamed Have Dinner – 40

Seven Poems from the Welsh – 42

The Toast – 45

The Natural and Social Sciences – 46

The Last Tea of Rikyu – 47

The Noh – 48

Inheritance – 49

The Origin of Geometry – 50

The Penitent – 51

The Don't Fall Inn – 52

Riddle – 53

Envoi – 54

ERRATA

I. Places in the Temple

Held – 59

Acts of Contrition – 60

The Incense Contest – 61

Glass – 64

The Commission – 65

Cruising Byzantium – 68

City of God – 69

Liverpool – 71

L – 72

Alas, Alice, – 73

A Discourse on Optics – 74

II. O'Ryan's Belt

The Hunter's Purse – 77

A Repertoire – 78

A Reprieve – 79

Theodora, Theodora – 80

Down – 81

The Classics – 82

III. True

The Chambers of Errors – 85

Reliquary – 86

Ovation – 87

Co-Pilot – 88

Cage, – 89

Meridian – 90

Lives of the Artists – 91

Signifyin' Monkey – 93

Shooting *The Crane People* – 95

Banzai – 96

Becoming Catastrophic – 97

True – 98

Privacy – 102

The Raindial – 103

The Brother – 104

Fraction – 105

Erratum – 106

Some Notes – 109

Acknowledgements

Shibboleth

Acknowledgement is gratefully made to the editors of the following periodicals, in which poems appeared: *Poetry Review, Poetry (Chicago), The Massachusetts Review, The Mississippi Review, The Chicago Review, Kansas Quarterly, Seneca Review, Orbis.*

'Machines' appeared as a limited edition designed by Barbara Tetenbaum, published by Circle Press Publications. 'Smith' appeared as a limited edition, also designed by Barbara Tetenbaum, and published by Triangular Press. 'Cadenza' was broadcast on *Poetry Now* (BBC Radio 3). 'Shibboleth' was also broadcast and appeared in pamphlet form as part of the 1987 National Poetry competition.

The quotation from Son House in 'Interviews' comes from Stefan Grossman's *Delta Blues Guitar*, Oak Publications, 1969.

Shibboleth replaces *Slivers* (Thompson Hill, Chicago, 1985) and includes revised versions of some of the poems in that collection.

Errata

Acknowledgements are gratefully made to the Arts Council of Great Britain, and to the editors of the following anthologies and periodicals in which some of these poems have appeared: the *Sunday Times, Poetry (Chicago)*, the *New Yorker*, the *New Statesman, Poetry Review*, the *Times Literary Supplement, The Honest Ulsterman, Verse, The Jacaranda Review, The Poetry Book Society Anthology 1991–1992.*

'Liverpool' was commissioned for BBC Radio's *Kaleidoscope* programme.

Several of the poems were first published by the Silver Buckle Press, University of Wisconsin–Madison Libraries, in a limited edition chapbook, *O'Ryan's Belt.*

SHIBBOLETH

Machines

Dearest, note how these two are alike:
This harpsichord pavane by Purcell
And the racer's twelve-speed bike.

The machinery of grace is always simple.
This chrome trapezoid, one wheel connected
To another of concentric gears,
Which Ptolemy dreamt of and Schwinn perfected,
Is gone. The cyclist, not the cycle, steers.
And in the playing, Purcell's chords are played away.

So this talk, or touch if I were there,
Should work its effortless gadgetry of love,
Like Dante's heaven, and melt into the air.

If it doesn't, of course, I've fallen. So much is chance,
So much agility, desire, and feverish care,
As bicyclists and harpsichordists prove

Who only by moving can balance,
Only by balancing move.

Pentecost

The neighbours hammered on the walls all night,
Outraged by the noise we made in bed.
Still we kept it up until by first light
We'd said everything that could be said.

Undaunted, we began to mewl and roar
As if desire had stripped itself of words.
Remember when we made those sounds before?
When we built a tower heavenwards
They were our reward for blasphemy.
And then again, two thousand years ago,
We huddled in a room in Galilee
Speaking languages we didn't know,
While amethyst uraeuses of flame
Hissed above us. We recalled the tower
And the tongues. We knew this was the same,
But love had turned the curse into a power.

See? It's something that we've always known:
Though we command the language of desire,
The voice of ecstasy is not our own.
We long to lose ourselves amid the choir
Of the salmon twilight and the mackerel sky,
The very air we take into our lungs,
And the rhododendron's cry.

And when you lick the sweat along my thigh,
Dearest, we renew the gift of tongues.

A Miracle

This will never do. Get the bird
Of gold enamelling out of the den.
I'm *reading*. Gin, white as winter sun,
Is blending juniper with oxygen.

Divinity is imminent. In the parlour
The crystal tinkling into words
Announces the arrival, through the mirror,
Of the host of stars and hummingbirds.

The angels have come early for the miracle.
They've gotten into the bar and drunk it dry.
Grinning, staggering, shedding feathers,
They can barely stand up, let alone fly.

One armoured, peacock-feathered cherub
Holds my copy of the future to the glass
And reads backwards (as they do in heaven)
Of how this evening will come to pass.

The seraphim are fencing on the lawn.
Thrust and parry, tipsy physical chess.
'The Conversation of the Blades', they call it,
The actual clink and whirr, the holiness.

Analysand

(Judges 12: 5–6)

I've had an important dream. But that can wait.
I want to talk about Ephraim Herrero
And the cobalt-blue tattoo of Mexico
That graced his arm above the wrist.

We were his disciples back in school.
The hours I spent echoing his accent,
Facing off to the mirror, smoothing my jacket
Over the bulge of a kitchen knife . . .

Once he held a razor to my throat . . .
But we've been over that a hundred times.
Did I tell you he won the Latin prize?
So you see it was more than contempt and fear

That drew us to him. The day that he got done
For selling envelopes of snow in May
Behind Our Lady of Guadaloupe
We were as much relieved as lost.

When the day of judgement came we were in court
Backing the loser, the soul of perjury
Wearing a tie he must have stolen from me
And someone else's Sunday suit.

It was a kick to see him so afraid.
And when he took the stand and raised his hand,
And his sleeve went south of the Rio Grande
I saw at once which side I was on.

Which brings me to the dream, if we have time.
I'm wading across a freezing river at night
Dressed in that suit and tie. A searchlight
Catches me mid-stream. I try to speak.

But someone steps between me and the beam.
The stars come out as if for an eclipse.
Slowly he raises his finger to his lips.
I wake before he makes that tearing sound.

More Machines

The clock of love? A smallish, round affair
That fits in the palm. A handy prop
Like any of these: compare
The pebble, the pearl, and the water drop.
They're all well made. But only one will prove
A fitting timepiece for our love.

To the pebble, the sun is a meteor,
The days a strobe, the years are swift.
Its machinery moves imperceptibly
Like the stars and continental drift.
But it's not for timing human love – it never *stops*.
Let us consider then the water drop

As it falls from the spigot during a summer storm
A distance of three feet. What does it see?
The lightning etched forever on the hot slate sky,
The birds fixed in an eternal V . . .
It falls so fast it knows no growth or changes.
A quick dog-fuck is all it measures

And it serves the beast as the stone serves God.
But our love doesn't hold with natural law.
Accept this small glass planet then, a shard
Grown smooth inside an oyster's craw.
Like us, it learns to opalesce
In darkness, in cold depths, in timelessness.

Deceit

The slate grey cloud comes up too fast.
The cornfield whispers like a fire.
The first drops strike and shake the stalks.
Desire attained is not desire.

The slate grey cloud comes up too fast.
However slyly we conspire,
The first drops strike and shake the stalks.
We cannot hold the thing entire.

The wind betrays its empty harvest.
The dead leaves spin and scratch the street,
Their longing for the forest
Forever incomplete.

Tell the driver to let you off
Around the corner. Be discreet.
Desire attained is not desire
But as the ashes of a fire.
The dead leaves spin and scratch the street.

The Present

For the present there is just one moon,
though every level pond gives back another.

But the bright disc shining in the black lagoon,
perceived by astrophysicist and lover,

is milliseconds old. And even that light's
seven minutes older than its source.

And the stars we think we see on moonless nights
are long extinguished. And, of course,

this very moment, as you read this line,
is literally gone before you know it.

Forget the here-and-now. We have no time
but this device of wantonness and wit.

Make me this present then: your hand in mine,
and we'll live out our lives in it.

Touch

We know she was clever because of her hands.
Hers, the first opposable thumb. Shards of her hip and skull
Suggest she was young, thirteen perhaps,
When the flash flood drowned her. Erect she stood
Lithe as a gymnast, four feet tall,

Our innocent progenitor.
Sleek-furred technician of flint and straw.
Here are her knuckle bones.

I know her touch. Though she could easily snap
My wrist, she is gentle in my dream.
She probes my face, scans my arm,
She touches my hand to know me.
Her eyes are grey in the dream, and bright.

Little mother, forgive me.
I wake you for answers in the night
Like any infant. Tell me about touch.
What necessities designed your hands and mine?
Did you kill, carve, gesture to god or gods?
Did the caress shape your hand or your hand the caress?

Music and Sex and Drinking

As a tripod stands more stable than a lectern
And lies threesquare to reason keeping level,
So three poles constitute us like dimensions:
The pebble is sexier than the owl, that drunkard,
And is all music after the final note.
All is mapped by music and sex and drinking.
Everything and each least part of everything
Each pole pulls to its own erasure
But is checked by the others,
So words keep their courtesies,
Stars keep their courses, nuclei cohere,
Till recklessly dislodged.

I find myself sobbing, over and over,
'I am exactly trivial and hold that everything,
And each least part of everything,
However tragic, chaste, tuneless, sober,
Can be accurately graphed upon these axes
To fill up its place in the world to the edges.'

'Smith'

What is this fear before the unctuous teller?
Why does it seem to take a forger's nerve
To make my signature come naturally?
Naturally? But every signature's
A trick we learn to do, consistently,
Like Queequeg's cross, or Whistler's butterfly.
Perhaps some childhood spectre grips my hand
Every time I'm asked to sign my name.

Maybe it's Sister Bridget Agatha
Who drilled her class in Christ and penmanship
And sneered *affected* at my seven-year-old scrawl.
True, it was unreadably ornate
And only one of five that I'd developed,
But try as I might I couldn't recall
The signature that I'd been born with.

Later, in my teens, I brought a girl,
My first, to see the Rodin exhibition.
I must have ranted on before each bronze;
Metal of blood and honey . . . Pure Sir Kenneth Clark.
And those were indeed the feelings I wanted to have,
But I could tell that she was unimpressed.
She fetched our coats. I signed the visitor's book,
My name embarrassed back into mere words.

No, I'm sure it all began years later.
I was twenty, and the girl was even younger.
We chose the hottest August night on record
And a hotel with no air-conditioning.
We tried to look adult. She wore her heels
And leant against the cigarette machine as,
Arching an eyebrow, I added to the register
The name I'd practised into spontaneity –
Surely it wasn't – *Mr and Mrs Smith*?

It's all so long ago and lost to me,
And yet, how odd, I remember a moment so pure,
In every infinite detail indelible,
When I gripped her small shoulders in my hands,
Steadying her in her slippery ride,
And I looked up into her half-closed eyes . . .
Dear friend, whatever is most true in me
Lives now and for ever in that instant,
The night I forged a hand, not mine, not anyone's,
And in that tiny furnace of a room,
Forged a thing unalterable as iron.

Cadenza

I've played it so often it's hardly me who plays.
We heard it that morning in Alexandria,
Or tried to, on that awful radio.
I was standing at the balustrade,
Watching the fish stalls opening on the quay,
The horizon already rippling in the heat.
She'd caught a snatch of Mozart, and was fishing
Through the static for the BBC
But getting bouzoukis, intimate Arabic,
All drowned beneath that soft roar, like the ocean's.
'Give it up,' I said, 'the tuner's broken.'
And then she crossed the room and kissed me. Later,
Lying in the curtained light, she whispered
She'd something to tell me. When all at once,
The tidal hiss we'd long since ceased to notice
Stopped. A flautist inhaled. And there it was,
The end of K285*a*,
Dubbed like a budget soundtrack on our big scene.
Next day I got the music out and learned it.

I heard it again in London a few months later,
The night she called me from the hospital.
'I've lost it,' she said, 'it happens . . .' and as she spoke
Those days in Egypt and other days returned,
Unsummoned, a tide of musics, cities, voices,
In which I drifted, helpless, disconsolate.
What did I mourn? It had no name, no sex,
'It might not even have been yours,' she said,
Or do I just imagine that she said that?

The next thing I recall, I'm in the dark
Outside St Michael's Church on Highgate Hill.
Coloured lights are strung across the portico,
Christmas lights. It's snowing on me,
And this very same cadenza – or near enough –
Rasps through a tubercular PA.
How did I get here?

Consider that radio, drifting through frequencies,
Suddenly articulate with Mozart.
Consider the soloist playing that cadenza,
Borne to the coda by his own hands.

Letter

It's stopped this morning, nine hours deep
And blank in the sun glare.
Soon the loud ploughs will drive through the drifts,
Spraying it fine as white smoke,
And give the roads back. Then I'll sleep
Knowing I've seen the blizzard through.

First your papers must be put in order.
In drawer after drawer your signatures wait
To wound me. I'll let them. There's nothing else in your hand.
No diaries, no labelled photographs, no lists.
But here's a letter you sent one year
With my name scratched carefully on onionskin.
Empty. Man of few words, you phoned to explain.
The only letter you ever wrote me
And you posted the envelope.

No relics here of how you felt;
Maybe writing frightened you, the way it fixed a whim.
Maybe ink and graphite made
Too rough a map of your fine love.
But remember one August night
When I was weak with fever and you held my head
And reeled off 'The Charge Of The Light Brigade'
(Of all things) to calm me. You had it by heart;
By breath. I'd hear that breath when you talked to yourself
Spitting tiny curses, or muttered in your sleep,
Or read, as monks and rabbis do, aloud, soft.
Breath that would hardly steam a mirror,
Whispering like gaslight. Day after year
After night I missed the words.

I always will. Of the funeral I recall
Only overcoats, a grey priest droning
'*The letter kills*', *said Paul*,
'*The spirit giveth life.*' And my breath,
Held, jaw clamped, the long drive home . . .

Three weeks have passed. Three weeks the clouds clenched
Low in the sky, too cold to snow until last night
When I rose to the slap of sleet on the glass and hard wind
And saw my face lamplit in the dark window,
Startled that I looked older, more like you.
Then half asleep, half frozen, close up against the pane, I
    mouthed
Father. Frost fronds quickly swirled and vanished
As if you read them back to me. Your breath
Making the blizzard silent,
The silence quiet, at last,
The quiet ours.

Shibboleth

One didn't know the name of Tarzan's monkey.
Another couldn't strip the cellophane
From a GI's pack of cigarettes.
By such minutiae were the infiltrators detected.

By the second week of battle
We'd become obsessed with trivia.
At a sentry point, at midnight, in the rain,
An ignorance of baseball could be lethal.

The morning of the first snowfall, I was shaving,
Staring into a mirror nailed to a tree,
Intoning the Christian names of the Andrews Sisters.
'Maxine, Laverne, Patty.'

Quorum

In today's *Guardian*, the word *quorum*
is spelled the same as *oqürum*,
the only surviving word of Khazar,
according to the *Great Soviet Encyclopaedia*.
Oqürum, meaning 'I have read'.

The original pronunciation is lost for ever,
but I weigh three syllables in my palm
against 'paprika' and 'samovar',
'cedarwood' and, for some reason,
'mistletoe'. I have read . . .

an entire literature,
and enacted all that it describes.
On a winter morning, in an ochre room
that we can never enter, the resonance
of those imaginary consonants

the elders whisper over ancient documents
flickers the blood bright shadow
from a glass of tea.

Auto da Fé

Last night I met my uncle in the rain
And he told me he'd been dead for fifty years.
My parents told me he'd been shot in Spain
Serving with the Irish volunteers.
But in this dream we huddled round a brazier
And passed the night in heated argument.
'El sueño de razón . . . ' and on it went.
And as he spoke he rolled a cigarette
And picked a straw and held it to an ember.
The shape his hand made sheltering the flame
Was itself a kind of understanding.
But it would never help me to explain
Why my uncle went to fight for Spain,
For Christ, for the Caudillo, for the King.

Ramon Fernandez?

I met him when I fought in the brigade,
In Barcelona, when the people had it.

Red flags snapped above the tower clock
Of what had been renamed the 'Lenin Barracks'.
The ancient face was permanently fixed,
If memory serves, at half eleven.
Dead right twice a day.

Fernandez played guitar each day at noon
In the plaza beneath the barracks tower,
Hawking his revolutionary broadsides.
And as he sang he stared up at the clock
As if he half expected it to move.

I recall the way he played the crowd
Sure as he played his lacquered blue guitar.
I recall the troop trains pulling from the station,
White knuckles over carbines, boys' voices
Singing the anthems of Ramon Fernandez.

And I wonder if anyone caught on but me.
The songs the fascists sang across the wire
Were his, the same he sang, got us to sing.
A few words changed, not many. *Libertad*,
Hermana Libre, I have them all by heart.

One day he vanished back across the front
And later, when the town was under siege,
A stray round hit the barracks clock and cracked
Both iron hands clean off but left the face
To glare like a phase of the moon above the burning city.

Partisans

Imagine them labouring selflessly,
Gathering evidence through the long winter.
Now they bring their case before you.
'Let us arrive at the truth together'

They say, these patient women and men.
The seconds tick by in the small cell.
The fluorescent bulb whines like a dentist's drill.
They want you to spell the names again.

Majority

Foreign policy does not exist for us.
We don't know where the new countries are.
We don't care. We want the streets safe
So we vote for the chair. An eye for an eye.

Our long boats will come in the spring
And we will take many heads.
The name of our tribe means 'human being'.
We will make your children pray to our god in public.

News item

The trampled corpses
Stacked in the lobby
Are all that remain of the literal-minded.

Among the missing
Are the little girl who shouted 'Fire'
And those of us who remained seated
Savouring the sheer
Theatre.

Pornography

The bodies of giants shine before us like a crowded fire.
One might quite credibly shout 'Theatre'.
I can't watch this. Instead, I'll stare at the projector beam
The smoke and dust revolve in and reveal.

Remember my story?
How one grey dawn in Maine I watched from my car
As a goshawk dove straight down toward the pines?
I said the dive was there before the hawk was,
Real as a wind shear before the blown snow reveals it.
The hawk became its aim, made one smooth purchase
In a splintering of twigs. A hare squealed, and I watched the bird
Slam the air in vain till it gave up and dropped its catch.
I told you how I sat and watched the rabbit die,
And described blood steaming on the frosted gravel.

Remember how angry you were
When I told you I'd made it up?
That I'd never been to Maine or owned a car?
But I told my tale well, bought your pity for the hare,
Terror for the hawk, and I served my point,
Whatever it was.

And remember that time
I was trapped in a cave and saw shadows on the limestone wall?
When the scouts freed me and carried me to the cave mouth
The true light burned my eyes like acid. Hours passed
Before I found myself safe in the Maine woods, resting in my car.

THE END is near. The final frame of *Triumph of the Will*
Slips past the lens and the blank flash blinds us.

26

Footage from the Interior

I

Boyoko is teaching me to wait.
We squat behind wrist-thick
Stalks of palm and listen
For the faint drumming of engines.

Just after sundown
The trawler slides around the headland.
The motor coughs, whinnies, and stops.
We watch and wait

As one by one the running lights
Go out across the dark lagoon.
Voices carry from the deck across the still water.
Not the words, but the sweep and glide of words.

Theirs is a tongue of tones and cadences
And Boyoko knows from the rhythm alone
Whether to slip away unseen
Or wait for rifles.

II

Boyoko is teaching me Lekele.
'Our word for *lagoon*
Can also mean *poison*, or *promise*,
Depending on the syllable stressed.'

A blue moth thrums
The windscreen of the idling jeep,
Slamming its tiny head against the glass
In urgent Morse.

Boyoko beats the word *freedom*
On the steering wheel.
'Try it.' I try it.
'No,' he tells me, 'you said *bacon*.'

III

Boyoko's been teaching me the 'talking drums'.
Side by side, we stand among the chickens
In the yard behind his hut.
I'm roasting. And my fingers ache.

Today when his son walked past
Boyoko lost me, slapping rhythm
Over rhythm. I stopped, he smiled,
And we resumed our lesson.

Minutes passed,
And then the boy came back
Bringing two cans of cold brown beer.

Khalypso

The development of complex cell communities in the zygote thus resembles the creation of heavier and heavier elements in the star's contraction ...

– R. Profitendieu, *Birth*

Cast off old love like substance from a flame;
Cast off that ballast from your memory.
But leave me and you leave behind your name.

When snows have made ideas of the rain,
When canvas bloats and ships grow on the sea,
Cast off old love like substance from a flame.

Your eyes are green with oceans and you strain
To crown and claim your sovereignty,
You leave me and you leave behind your name

And all the mysteries these isles retain.
But if the god of sailors hacks you free,
Cast off old love like substance from a flame

Until you're in a woman's bed again
And make her moan as you make me,
'Leave me and you leave behind your name.'

The brails go taut. The halyard jerks, the pain
Of breeching to the squall and all to be
Cast off, old love, like substance from a flame.
Now leave me. I will live behind your name.

The Bacchae

Look out, Slim, these girls are trouble.
You dance with them they dance you back.
They talk it broad but they want it subtle
and you got too much mouth for that.
Their secret groove's their sacred grove –
not clever not ever, nor loud, nor flaunt.
I know you, Slim, you're a jerk for love.
The way you talk is the what you want.
You want numbers. You want names.
You want to cheat at rouge et noir.
But these are initiated dames –
the how they move is the what they are.

A Disaster

We were ships in the night.
We thought her rockets were fireworks.

Our radio was out, and we didn't know
The band was only playing to calm the passengers.

Christ, she was lovely all lit up,
Like a little diamond necklace!

Try to understand. Out here in the dark
We thought we were missing the time of our lives.

We could almost smell her perfume.
And she went down in sight of us.

Starlet

Berenice affects her April dialect.
Buds bloom stiffly to her rapid vowels, mud breaks
For apple-green shoots. Nude, descending
A staircase, she trails a shady wake of geometries
Like a ship stirring shoals of luminous algae.
Freely she warms to the folk whose soles
Thump brownly on her marble floors.
She breathes their garlic air wheezed
From hot concertinas and, in the cool evening,
She unbinds her starry skein of hair,
The heavens bespangling with dishevelled light,
Gives interviews.

Interviews

Yvette lets a drop
Of red blot brilliant
On the white,
Fresh bedsheet.

1913. She looks up
From painting her toenails.
Marcel is ahead of his time,
Yvette is still dressing.

He finds a note
From Apollinaire:
'Knight to
Queen's rook three.'

And checks the board.
He looks at the little horse, snaps
It across the room,
A distance

> *Of fifty years*
> *To a studio in Neuilly*
> *Cassette wheels spinning*
> *Throughout the interview*
> *And he thinks of bicycles.*

Q: *Where does your anti-retinal attitude come from?*
A: *From too great an importance given to the retina.*

1913. It's getting late.
The sun obscures
As it illuminates
Garden and gardener
Whose hedge-clippers snip . . .

'Zip me,'
Yvette says over her shoulder,
Stepping into her yellow pumps,

The ones with the goldfish in the heels.

> *Wait, I'll flip*
> ~~*The cassette to erase*~~
> *'Interview with Delta bluesman*
> *Son House 1/5/68'*

Q: *What about Willie, was he very good at making up verses?*
A: *Yeh, he could make up verses pretty good. Yeh, 'cause he'd start on one thing he'd let near about every word be pertaining to what he pronounced what he was going to play about. That's the difference in him and Charley and me, too. Charley, he could start singing of the shoe there and wind up singing about that banana.*

Marcel looks at the little horse
And wonders whether
'Nude Descending a Staircase'
Is the name of his entry
In the armoury show

Or if 'Nude Descending a Staircase'
Is his entry
In the armoury show.

Within three years
His friends will drop in the trench
Screaming, chlorine searing
Their throats and noses raw.
Apollinaire in the field-hospital,
Red on white gauze,
Will imagine the random trajectories
Of fragments, shrapnel, chessmen.

A: *Since Courbet, it's been believed that painting is addressed to the retina. Before, painting had other functions: it could be ... moral.*

Stop.

I'd be playin' by myself sometime, nobody will be around me whatever to hear it, and my mind will be settin' on some crazy things – Scripture or jes names of songs, any old thing. 'Fore I know anything tears'll be coming down and I put that guitar away.

Back from the Salon,
Yvette removes
Her yellow shoes.
The gramophone
Clears its throat
For Satie.

Yvette, Yvette,
So much to drink.

From tonight on you'll be Rrose,
Rrose Selavy.

Later he'll undress her.
Setting long glove

And stocking down at right
Angles. Here comes

The bride.

> *Duchamp then produced*
> *A miniature machine for me*
> *To photograph: watch parts*
> *Clicking and skidding*
> *Across clear, flat glass*
> *Toward two gnat-sized yellow shoes.*

But now they laugh in the dark.
Lighting her cigarette,

Marcel makes a world around them,
A short, shining world.

Remembering Steps to Dances
Learned Last Night

Massive my heart, the heart of a hero, I knew it,
Though I was ten, pimpled, squint eyed, dung spattered.
I strung a bow, and memorized a brief heroic song
(I'll sing it for you later), left my goats in my father's yard,
And then went down to the ship.
Many men massed at the dock, loud their laughter.
But the king listened, noted my name, gave me wine,
A little patriotic speech, and sent me home
To the goats and the tedium and the ruminant years.
Once I made a song about the king and his distant plundering
And the hoard of memories, wondrous, he was gathering.
It's a shame you didn't bring your guitar.

Then one summer, when I was older,
And the king was long since missing in action,
Men came from Achaia to court the lonely queen.
The nights got loud with drums and laughter echoing from the
    palace,
Women's laughter, and the smell of roasted lamb.
What would you have done? I pounded on the gates one
    morning,
Rattled my arrows and stamped and sang about my hero-heart.
They seemed to understand . . . Or didn't mind my lying,
And they opened the gates on another world.
Beauty. Deception. Of weaving, of magic, and of the edge of
    the known world
When the light fails, and you fall dead drunk across the table,
All these we learned in our feasts and games amid the grey-
    eyed women.
Clever men and many we waited, the queen to choose among.

I know you came to hear me sing about the night the king came
    home,
When hero slaughtered hero in the rushlit hall,
Blood speckling the white clay walls wine dark.
I can't. I'd stepped outside when the music stopped mid-tune.
Alone in the dark grove, I heard no sound but distant insects,
And the sound of water, mine, against the palace wall.
And then I heard their screams, the men and women I'd spent
    that summer with.

What would you have done?
I staggered home in the dawn rain, still half drunk,
Forgetting one by one the names of my dead friends,
Remembering steps to dances learned that night,
that very night,
Back to my goats, goat stink, goat cheese, the governing of
    goats.

The Tuning

If anyone asks you how I died, say this:
The angel of death came in the form of a moth
And landed on the lute I was repairing.
I closed up shop
And left the village on the quietest night of summer,
The summer of my thirtieth year,
And went with her up through the thorn forest.

Tell them I heard yarrow stalks snapping beneath my feet
And heard a dog bark far off, far off.
That's all I saw or heard,
Apart from the angel at ankle level leading me,
Until we got above the beeline and I turned
To look for the last time on the lights of home.

That's when she started singing.
It's written that the voice of the god of Israel
Was the voice of many waters.
But this was the sound of trees growing,
The noise of a pond thrown into a stone.

When I turned from the lights below to watch her sing,
I found the angel changed from moth to woman,
Singing inhuman intervals through her human throat,
The notes at impossible angles justified.

If you understand, friend, explain to them
So they pray for me. How could I go back?
How could I bear to hear the heart's old triads –
Clatter of hooves, the closed gate clanging,
A match scratched toward a pipe –
How could I bear to hear my children cry?

I found a rock that had the kind of heft
We weigh the world against
And brought it down fast against my forehead
Again, again, until blood drenched my chest
And I was safe and real forever.

Rational Construction

Along a girder, high above the pavement
A man is carrying a man-length mirror.
Crowds gather to track his movements,
His one foot easing over the other.
We squint, and the sun snaps down from the glass
Finding faces. But up there they keep
Their eyes on their feet. We bask in their flash,
But they owe us no 'intuitive leap'.

The Dreamer and the Dreamed
Have Dinner

Rien n'est, en effet, plus désenchantant, plus pénible, que de regarder, après des années, ses phrases. Elles se sont en quelque sorte décantées et déposées au fond du livre; et, la plupart du temps les volumes ne sont pas ainsi que les vins qui s'améliorent en vieillissant; une fois dépouillés par l'âge, les chapitres s'éventent, et leur bouquet s'étiole.

– Huysmans

It is the ripest hour. He stands before the window,
Scans the night and sighs, clouding the pane.
Road. Streetlamps. Shops. The solstice light
Smooths a pool of similes disguised as names.
His carafe, half drained, opaque in the dark,
Conceals before it is uncorked and poured.
Beyond mere sense, so does his heart
Until the clock, clicks locked in random clusters,
Resolves arhythmically. Chuck: a car door?
'Her Citroën,' he thinks, because he trusts her
Cycles and her secret female arts.
All wines retain impurities. A sip
Numbs an unexamined intention as she knocks.
His welcomes are readied with overkill workmanship.

'Late again.' They talk. They spend the twilight
On his terrace rereading *Against the Grain.*
'Like tears in different colours . . .' (She *abhors*
It when he does this. Large drops of warm rain
Dapple their shoulders, so they drift indoors.)
She stretches and yawns; he persists unaware . . .
'Like gazing at a photographic detail
Of a wineglass, unable to say what it is.'
Why must he slow the sunset with these flares?

'Oh for a beaker full of the warm south,'
She offers. Stumped, he laughs for sheer decorum.
Nothing slowly happens. Their shadows stretch out
In a half-light charged with visionary boredom:
Pale whims, faint furies, dim endeavours
Await the age's end, the commonsense of darkness.
When will darkness come? When will the lovers?

Seven Poems from the Welsh

Sion ap Brydydd (d. 1360) was a contemporary of the undisputed master of classical Welsh poetry, Dafydd ap Gwilym, and it is in the shadow of Dafydd's achievement that Sion's significance has been so unfortunately obscured. A commoner by birth, Sion borrowed a sum from the court of Owain for his education to the career of court poet. He held that post for less than a year when he was dismissed for neglecting to repay the loan and he spent his remaining years among the criminal element of Aberystwyth. Perhaps as a result, his diction is a mixture of poetic 'mandarin' Welsh and earthy demotic. And this, together with his obsessive use of difficult forms, has marked him as an eccentric in the history of Welsh poetry. For example, recent computer analysis of *Y Hiraeth*, his 30,000-word description of the interior of a heron's egg, has revealed two columns of slant rhyme weaving through the text line by line in a perfect double helix pattern. How such a poem could have been written under such exacting formal constraints is a puzzle. Why it was written is a positive enigma.

He is best known, however, for his 30-syllable *englynion*. These short poems were not *composed* in the sense in which that term applies to the writing of English poetry. Rather, they were thought to have *obtained*, like Japanese *tanka* and *haiku*, as the complete and inevitable response to a split second of painfully acute perception. To the objection that the preconceived form of the poem shapes that perception, Sion would answer that during such moments neither poet, poem, nor subject can be distinguished one from the other. In this mysterious way, he believed, all his englynion were faint echoes of a single unwritten poem which, if pronounced, would so perfectly unite the souls of author and listener that they would inhabit each other's bodies and exchange destinies. This poem, he believed, drifted just beyond his grasp 'like a snowflake of complex geometry which dissolves when it lights on the tongue'.

In the winter of 1360 Sion was beheaded for the crime of adultery. Here are my translations of seven in a sequence of twenty-nine englynion he wrote in the tower of Pentraeth on the eve of his execution.

I

Morfydd, daughter of Gwyn,
The dells are bright with snow.
Driven with cruel purity,
They'll take you for one of their own.

II

Cloves and cedar smoke in the air,
Swarms of dragonflies in the long grass.
I unlaced her muslin gown.
No help from her.

III

Smooth the skin on a bowl of milk
And on the warm hollow of her thigh.
The soft turf is slow to warm,
And after this, shallow breathing.

IV

The moment you touch the whorl of my ear
With the tip of your tongue
Is a gold dome over itself.
So is the moment after.

XXVII

Dull the journey.
Feeble and muttering the old men.
Amber and sweet the wine of spring.
I won't have autumn's vinegar.

XXVIII

Dull the journey.
Long the road reeled in toward the lantern.
Patience is cold soup
And salt in the sugar bowl.

XXIX

Say this rhyme, reader, aloud to yourself.
Gladly I'd bear your senility and incontinence,
Let you warm this bed of hay,
Rattle these chains, write these lines.

The Toast

You may have glimpsed a version of the Toast – our most curious tradition – played by our children on the streets of your cities at twilight, or seen, at our weddings, the young men dressed in red shot silk, wineglasses balanced brim-full on the backs of their hands, shuffling the intricate steps whilst reciting the tongue-twisting parable of the tailor's thimble.

The age and meaning of the Toast are much disputed. Heraklius contends that the ritual is merely a corruption of a trick schoolboys once used to remember the names and dates of our country's defeats. It will be noted that Heraklius is a northerner. A more promising avenue of investigation lies in the fact that, 'the thimble', familiar to us from the nursery as part of the dandling-song of the infant prince exposed on the hillside and raised by fieldmice, is in fact a rebus for remembering the constellations, and the accurate dancing of the toast was a skill much prized among our seafaring ancestors who chanted the story to navigate, stomping the deckboards and raising ladles of fresh water to the Pole Star.

And it was said to be once a trial for witches or spies from the north who, unable to mimic the nimble steps and rhymes would trip up, drop the chalice, and seal their fates. And some scholars say that the story is only a code for the steps of another dance, long since forgotten, but often depicted in the *goblet-bearing youth* motif of our pottery.

The Natural and Social Sciences

We come to Straidkilly to watch the tide go out.
A man is loading a wicker basket
With small, complicated pink crabs.
'Have we missed it,' we ask, 'the tide?'
And he, with sincere assurance,
'It'll be back.'

A girl inspects an upside-down bike
On the road to Tubbercurry.
I stop to help but she rights it on its wheels,
Shoves off, ticking in the light rain.

Musicians in the kitchen, Sunday morning in Gweedore.
An American with a tape recorder and a yellow notebook.
'What was the name of that last one?'
The piper shrugs and points to the dark corner.
'Ask my father.'
The American writes 'Ask My Father'.

The Last Tea of Rikyu

Early evening and a summer presence.
A moist wind moves on the roofs of Horyu-Ji,
Flicks iridescent beetle wings beneath wrought copper;
It is the daily rainstorm.

But we are in the tea hut in Rikyu's garden.
Rikyu, slandered without grace or respect,
Condemned by a dull and intolerant patron,
Is granted an hour of life.

The whirr of insects,
The master's hands, the lanterns,
And the damp hiss of the kettle
Show forth from the moment.

We take our places.
        'Do not be sad.
        We will meet every time there is tea.'
The unsteady cup warms my hands.

The others withdraw like shadows.
I remain to witness the gesture.
Rikyu unwraps bands of black silk
From the short sword.

His eyes are clear.
        'Have we not already died
        Who live beyond fear and desire?'
I weep for humility and gratitude

And do not see the shock, the body buckling.
This is how it always begins;
A jolt, the world whirls within us,
A raindrop hesitates, then hits the roof.

The Noh

After 1868 when the Shogunate was overthrown and the Noh fell out of favour, the costumers and mask makers who had previously produced so many rich effects became careless in their productions, offering only a few crude variations.

– Yamashiro, *A History of Noh*

From the bright glass greenhouse steamed with palms
She brings you from sleep to where she has tacked
A mask of wood to a trellis arm
To seduce you. She *is* abstract.

Thunderstorms tonight, she warns.
No stars suspend above the palms
But gro-lights crackle on the leathery leaves.
Tonight, in her arms,

Conquer the noble opacity of the mask
Back to its maker who planed the cheapest wood
Against the grain and pilfered the design
Arse deep in debt and carving against a deadline.

His early masks were perfect. So were mine.
But roles come and go, standards and wood decay
And split. One can no longer say,
'Had we but world enough and time',

You just make do. Unclench your fists.
This delicate cheek and skin of painted pine
Provide your mind for silence by themselves.
He taught no truth to shape who chiselled this.

The gong tolls classically. It is twelve,
And the drops against the glass become a hiss.
Kiss her. Her rhythmic breathing levels
Beyond her name and beauty to a 'yes'.
Together leave the greenhouse its emptiness.

Inheritance

My father would have cherished an heir,
but he remained unmarried.

Science was his mistress, and after science,
my mother. But we were provided

with a collection of seashells
second only to the emperor's.

I regret I will not live
to see the final specimen auctioned.

It is the jewel in the diadem.
A sulphur nautilus,

wound like the spring of a gold watch.
My mother would not part with it in life.

When he died I saw his name
in the *Journal of Marine Genetics*. Sharp,

peach-coloured spikes of coral
are named for him.

The Origin of Geometry

High above Thebes the huge birds glide
Describing smaller and smaller circles.
Below, the Greek boy tells his teacher

That all things, the cinnamon air at dusk
And the red sand, are the 3D
Writing of the gods.

Just so, he says, his alphabet's a world
Dug in red sand with a cypress stick.
He stands above it like a god.

But the old man carves pictures
On a lump of clay. Moon. Scarab.
'See? See?' Young Thales points

To the first letter of his name.
'Round like the moon.' The old man squints
Brushing a fly from his face.

In just a moment
They will lose the gods for ever.
But now the cranes fly round and round

Into the maelstrom of the lengthening light.

The Penitent

At times also I have been put to confusion and driven to despair of ever explaining something for which I could not account, but which my senses told me to be true.

– Galileo Galilei, *Two New Sciences*

Unseen, dogs cough on the colourless beach
Over waves, incessant, incessant. If all this sand
Were dried and ground and polished to a lens
That order now fanned out too far
For us to see could focus through it.
But see, they subside, Procyon and the Twins.
Defaced by day, their imagined musculature
Crushes and sharpens a tiny brilliance on my sin,
Igniting kindling. My eyes are stung with smoke;
Too much truth in too grey a place
And too combustible a heart. These days
I move in quiet circles and take for nourishment
Light's white gristle, the unprismed lie.
God shines. The tide looks solid in his love,
And yet it *does* move.

The Don't Fall Inn

The blue pool illuminated, the cocktail lounge is open.
Rippling with liquid glints like firelight,
The lit bellhop gazes in terror
At the diving board and the cool, deep mirror.

Here is the Register of Revelations.
Use my pen. 'Edvard . . . and . . . Mimi . . . Munch.'
We hear muffled voices through the walls.
A strangely submarine effect. Like bubbles.

Something is terribly wrong
And the porters come to dust it.
They are hoovering as we leave at dawn.
Although the word 'TV' is out,
They flash the sign against the hail grey sky:
REASONABLE RATES   OLYMPIC SIZE POOL
                    . . . IN EVERY ROOM

Goodbye.

Riddle

I am the book you'll never read
But carry
For ever,

One blunt page, garlanded
By daughter
Or lover.

You already know two-thirds by heart.
And I'm passing weighty for a work so short.

Envoi

Go away. All that's over.
No more fluttering, squirming, crawling, running.
I've achieved stillness, clarity.
Since the tide gave up this one rock
And I'm the only point to reckon by
Many of you have taken me for a sign.
Stop. Stay on the deep.
Wing back down the round sleep of waters.
Deceive them, tell them it never ends.
Give me peace.

But the speech of skulls is strange to birds.
Weary, eager for crumbs and Noah's praise,
The dove snapped half the glittering twig
Curling green in the eye socket,
Clutched it, flew.

ERRATA

I. Places in the Temple

Held

Not in the sense that this snapshot, a girl in a garden,
Is named for its subject, or saves her from ageing,
Not as this ammonite changed like a sinner to minerals
Heavy and cold on my palm is immortal,
But as we stopped for the sound of the lakefront one morning
Before the dawn chorus of sprinklers and starlings.

Not as this hieroglyph chiselled by Hittites in lazuli,
Spiral and faint, is a word for 'unending',
Nor as the hands, crown, and heart in the emblem of Claddagh,
Pewter and plain on that ring mean forever,
But as we stood at the window together, in silence,
Precisely twelve minutes by candlelight waiting for thunder.

Acts of Contrition

There's you, behind the red curtain,
waiting to absolve me in the dark.
Here's me, third in the queue outside
the same deep green velvet curtain.
I'm working on my confessional tone.

Here's me opening my wrists
before breakfast, Christmas day,
and here's you asking if it hurt.
Here's where I choose between *mea culpa*
and *Why the hell should I tell you?*

Me again, in the incident room this time,
spitting my bloody teeth into your palm.
I could be anyone you want me to be.
I might come round to your point of view.

The Incense Contest

Are you awake, my sweet barbarian?
Why, you look as though you'd seen a ghost!
Are you so shocked to see a lady smoke?
I owe this habit to the Prince, my husband.
That interests you? But that was years ago,
When high-born women told the time by crickets
And generals burned perfumes in their helmets
The night before they rode their troops to battle.
Among the rich it was considered proper
For gentlemen to keep some trace of court
About them in the sweat and shit and smoke.
Among our set those days, in fact, the game
Of 'Guess the Incense' was the latest rage.
Played, like all our games, in grace and earnest,
By intricate directions, for high stakes.

And crispest winter evenings were the best
Because the air is cleanest in the cold.
Without music, badinage, or flowers,
With all attention focused on the flame,
We'd kneel and sniff, and sigh in recognition,
Or we'd pretend, to save a reputation,
Or gamble on assent when someone twigged
'Why this is *Plum Tree Blossom* mixed with balsam.'
On such a night the Empress proposed
An incense contest for the Heian ladies.

We worked for weeks refining subtleties
Of clove and cinnamon and sandalwood,
Selecting lacquers for the bowls and burners
And stiff kimonos for our serving girls.
Imagine generals in midnight camps
Nudging sticks and pebbles across maps;
Just so we worried over strategies
Until the evening of the second snow.

That night we drank the Empress's *sake*.
The Prince, my husband, danced and spoke
A poem written by my grandfather:

> *Shadows on your screens;*
> *a document inked in script*
> *I will yet master.*

A very famous poem. You smile, my lord,
But I come from a literary line.

The alcove, I recall, was full of courtiers
Brushing snow from silken hunting vests
And ladies hushing them. A fan was flicked
To signify the contest had commenced.

First my cousin knelt above the brazier
And blent two scents together on the fire.
Eagles in Winter Light, I think,
And *Village of the Pines* with bergamot.
At first I found her effort elegant,
Warm and old and calm. But moments later,
Barbed and pungent with an old resentment.
The Empress nodded, and glancing toward my husband
Misquoted one of my grandfather's lines.

Next my sister burnt an amber resin
Suggesting pavements after summer rain.
We all felt something which we couldn't name
But which we all agreed was sad and cold
And distant, like some half-remembered grief
From girlhood, or a herb like marjoram.
Once more her Majesty addressed the Prince,
'You seem to have remarkably broad taste.'
And looked at me with something worse than pity.
I knew I'd lost. And when it was my turn
To add my clichéd fragrance to the fire
A door slid open deep within my head . . .

But how can I describe what happened then?
Except to say the blind must dream. They smell
And touch and taste and hear; and you, my dear,
Can dream – are dreaming even now, perhaps –
While all about you swirls a hidden world
Where memories contend like hungry ghosts.
I didn't smell my incense in the brazier:
I smelled the forest and I smelled the horses,
The dung in stables, women giving birth,
The rotting teeth of footmen from the provinces,
The coppery reek of blood, the clogged latrines,
The foetid corpses of the foreign priests
My husband crucified at Gyotoku.
I smelled so many women on the Prince
I smelled the Prince on every woman there.

Are you awake? For if it please you, lord,
To hold that candle just beneath my pipe
Until the black tar glows . . .
                              There. I smoke
To keep those smells at bay. It isn't free,
My dear barbarian, so don't forget
To demonstrate that generosity
For which your noble race is celebrated.
The crickets signal dawn. Time to rise
And face the sun and leave me to my dream.

Glass

This is a cheapjack gift at the year's end.
This is a double-glazing hymn for wind.
This is a palm frond held out to a friend
Who holds her lifeline lightly in her hand.

As fine sand filaments the unclenched hand
Or leaves the palm grit-filmed but crazed, lines end
Across prismatic windscreens. Every friend
A meteorologist's diagram of wind.

Blow smoke into the fist of either hand
And pull it tight and loop it round the end
Of every night held up by wine and friend,
Sootflecked and leaning on a London wind,

Then say our ribboned smoke's erased by wind,
Our glass is sand. You start, but in the end,
Somehow, I stay. You stay, somehow, my friend
Who grips me tightest in her open hand.

The Commission

In spring when the mountain snows melt
and the western wind crumbles
and loosens the clods, in the spring
when the bees roam incontinently
over the glades and the woodlands,
I returned to the plague-levelled city
to cut off the head of the man
who had murdered my brother.

To cover my purpose and pay off my debts
I set up a shop in the Via Rigoglio
and accepted a papal commission.
In the evenings I shadowed
the arquebusier Ludovico
like a love-smitten boy,
watching his house,
his comings and goings.

Pope Clement had ordered three follies:
a spindly gold locust that chirruped and kicked
on release of a mainspring,
an amethyst brooch,
and a nine-inch stiletto
with monogrammed handle in findrinny
and he wanted a cameo laid in its pommel:
Hercules binding the three-headed Cerberus.

To help me I hired a silversmith
known as Filippo, whose idiot daughter
I kept in the shop to amuse me. But
during that summer she fell in a fever.
Her hand was diseased. Both the bones of her thumb
and ring finger were eaten away.
I'd received an advance from the Pope
so I sent for the finest of surgeons.

She screamed when he started
to scrape away some of the bone
using a crude iron tool, and since
I could see he was making no progress
I got him to stop for five minutes. I ran
to the workshop and fashioned
a delicate instrument, steel, curved,
tiny and sharp as a razor.

This I gave to the surgeon
who now worked so gently
the girl felt no pain.
Filippo in gratitude made me a gift
of a dagger he'd chanced on in Persia.
He knew I would find the design on the handle
compelling – the name of their god
swirling like silvery foliage.

(The ignorant call such engravings 'grotesques'
because they resemble the carvings in grottoes.
This is an error. For just as the ancients
created their monsters
by mating with bulls and with horses,
so we artists create our own monsters
in networks of intertwined branches and leaves.)

I finally found Ludovico alone
on the night of the feast of St Mark.
It was pissing down rain and the bells
of S. Paolo were striking eleven.
I crept up behind as he stood
in a doorway in Torre Sanguigna
and brought down the silversmith's dagger
as hard as I could on his nape

but he turned and I shattered his shoulder.
Blinded with pain he let go of his sword
and again I went straight for his neck,
and this time the blade stuck so deep that it snapped
at the hilt. Then he fell to his knees
and stared at me stupidly, clutching the knife
as if he were trying to keep me away from it.
I looked in his eyes until I was sure they were empty.
Then footsteps. I broke off the handle and ran.

I was suspected of course, so I kept out of sight
and worked day and night for the Pope
as I had no desire to spend August in Rome
or get myself hanged.
When I finally brought him his toys
he was propped up in bed
being bled. But he granted an audience.
Jaundice. His flesh was like cheese.

When I laid out my labours before him
he squinted and sent for his spectacles,
then for more lamps. But it was no use.
He was blind as a mole.
Most of the time he spent sighing
and praising my God-given talent,
thumbing that wretched mechanical insect.

He almost ignored the stiletto
on which, from the figure of Hercules down,
I'd copied the Persian device from the dagger
that brought me such luck, disguising
the writing as branches.

By Christmas Pope Clement was dead.
And all of my efforts to stay in his favour
were wasted, which just goes to show
how completely the stars rule our lives.

Cruising Byzantium

The saved, say firemen, sometimes return,
Enduring the inferno of the flat
To fetch the family photos. And they burn
Not for cash, cashmere coat, nor cat,
Nor, as they momently suppose, for love.
They perish for the heraldries of light
And not such lives as these are emblem of.
But the saved, say firemen, are sometimes right.

Have you seen our holiday snaps from Greece?
Each Virgin burns in incandescent wonder
From her gold mosaic altarpiece.
This one was smashed by Gothic boot boys under
Orders from an Emperor who burned
The icon painters for idolatry.
Before her ruined face the faithful learned
The comet's path to a celestial sea.
And look. Here's *you* in skintight scuba gear
Winking through the window of your mask!
You have become the fetish that you wear.
I know precisely what you're going to ask;
Though golden in the Adriatic haze
You've waded to your thighs in molten light,
Your second skin aglitter in the sprays,
Your first it was we brought to bed that night.
And yet I'd almost brave the flames to keep
This idyll of perversity from burning.

Each photo frames a door beyond which, deep
Within the Patriarchate of my yearning,
The marble pavements surge with evensong.
But firemen say the saved are sometimes wrong.

City of God

When he failed the seminary he came back home
to the Bronx and sat in a back pew
of St Mary's every night reciting the Mass
from memory – quietly, continually –
into his deranged overcoat.
He knew the local phone book off by heart.
He had a system, he'd explain,
perfected by Dominicans in the Renaissance.

To every notion they assigned a saint,
to every saint an altar in a transept of the church.
Glancing up, column by column, altar by altar,
they could remember any prayer they chose.
He'd used it for exams, but the room went wrong –
a strip-lit box exploding slowly as he fainted.
They found his closet papered floor to ceiling
with razored passages from St Augustine.

He needed a perfect cathedral in his head,
he'd whisper, so that by careful scrutiny
the mind inside the cathedral inside the mind
could find the secret order of the world
and remember every drop on every face
in every summer thunderstorm.
And that, he'd insist, looking beyond you,
is why he came home.

I walked him back one evening as the snow
hushed the precincts of his vast invisible temple.
Here was Bruno Street where Bernadette
collapsed, bleeding through her skirt
and died, he had heard, in a state of mortal sin;

here, the site of the bakery fire where Peter stood
screaming on the red-hot fire escape,
his bare feet blistering before he jumped;
and here the storefront voodoo church beneath the el
where the Cuban *bruja* bought black candles,
its window strange with plaster saints and seashells.

Liverpool

Ever been tattooed? It takes a whim of iron,
takes sweating in the antiseptic-stinking parlour,
nothing to read but motorcycle magazines
before the blood-sopped cotton and, of course, the needle,
all for – at best – some Chinese dragon.
But mostly they do hearts,

hearts skewered, blurry, spurting like the Sacred Heart
on the arms of bikers and sailors.
Even in prison they get by with biro ink and broken glass,
carving hearts into their arms and shoulders.
But women's are more intimate. They hide theirs,
under shirts and jeans, in order to bestow them.

Like Tracy, who confessed she'd had hers done
one legless weekend with her ex.
Heart. Arrow. Even the bastard's initials, R.J.L.,
somewhere where it hurt, she said,
and when I asked her where, snapped 'Liverpool'.

Wherever it was, she'd had it sliced away
leaving a scar, she said, pink and glassy,
but small, and better than having his mark on her,

(that self-same mark of Valentinus,
who was flayed for love, but who never
– so the cardinals now say – existed.
Desanctified, apocryphal, like Christopher,
like the scar you never showed me, Trace,
your (   ), your ex, your 'Liverpool').

Still, when I unwrap the odd anonymous note
I let myself believe that it's from you.

L

'Switch off the engine and secure the car.'
He slots his pen across his clipboard
and makes a little cathedral of his fingers
as though I were helping him with his enquiries.
'Tell me, Michael, what's your line of work?'

I tell him the truth. Why not? I've failed anyway.
'Driving and writing have a lot in common,'
he parleys, and we sit there, the two of us
blinking into the average braking distance
for 30 mph, wondering what he means.

I want to help but it's his turn to talk.
When my turn comes he'll probably look at me
instead of his hand, stalled now in mid-gesture
like a milkfloat halfway across a junction.
Look at him. What if I'd said *butcher*?

At last 'It's all a matter of giving – proper – signals'
is the best he can do. But then he astonishes me.
'I'm going to approve your licence,
but I don't care much for your . . .' Quick glance.
'*interpretation* of the Highway Code.'

Alas, Alice,

who woke to crows and woke up on the ceiling and hung there fearing the evening's sweeping and looked down now at her unfinished reading and loved by sleeping and slept by weeping and called out once. The words were dust. Who left late singing and signed up leaving and ran home slowly afraid of sleeping and hated thinking and thought by feeling and called out once but no one came,

who dreamt blue snow and froze in dreaming and spoke by reading and read all evening and read by patterns of blizzards drifting and dared by waiting and waited taking and called out once and called out twice and coughed grey clouds and carved four coffins and took by thanking and thanked by seeking and drifted bedwards and lay there weeping and counted her tears and divided by seven and called out once. The words were crows.

A Discourse on Optics

i. The Heirloom

Now its silver paint is flaking off,
That full-length antique bevelled mirror
Wants to be clear water in a trough,
Still, astringent water in November.

It worked for sixty years, day and night
Becoming this room and its passing faces.
Holding it now against the light
I see the sun shines through in places.

It wants to be the window that it was,
Invisible as pleasure or pain,
Framing whatever the day may cause –
The moon. A face. Rain.

I'll prop it up outside against the skip
So clouds can ghost across the rust.
Though I can't see myself in it,
Still, it's the only mirror that I trust.

ii. The Pond

The shape of man, a shadow on the ground,
Returns, a mirror image, from pondwater.
So it is we think the soul not shade,
Not silhouette, but solid matter.

Except those times light strikes the basin level
And almost makes a window of the surface
To show our shadow amid coins and gravel
Outgazing the sad overcoat and face,

To teach them, I suppose, they are that darkness
Deepening the bottom of the pool,
And teach the soul it wears the face and coat
Which that lucidity obscures.

II. O'Ryan's Belt

The Hunter's Purse

is the last unshattered 78
by 'Patrolman Jack O'Ryan, violin',
a Sligo fiddler in dry America.

A legend, he played Manhattan's ceilidhs,
fell asleep drunk one snowy Christmas
on a Central Park bench and froze solid.
They shipped his corpse home, like his records.

This record's record is its lunar surface.
I wouldn't risk my stylus to this gouge,
or this crater left by a flick of ash –

When Anne Quinn got hold of it back in Kilrush,
she took her fiddle to her shoulder
and cranked the new Horn of Plenty
Victrola over and over and over,
and scratched along until she had it right
or until her father shouted

> 'We'll have *no* more
> Of *that* tune
> In *this* house to*night.*'

She slipped out back and strapped the contraption
to the parcel rack and rode her bike
to a far field, by moonlight.

It skips. The penny I used for ballast slips.
O'Ryan's fiddle pops, and hiccoughs
back to this, back to this, back to this:
a napping snowman with a fiddlecase;
a flask of bootleg under his belt;
three stars; a gramophone on a pushbike;
a cigarette's glow from a far field;
over and over, three bars in common time.

A Repertoire

'Play us one we've never heard before'
we'd ask this old guy in our neighborhood.
He'd rosin up a good three or four
seconds, stalling, but he always could.
This was the Bronx in 1971,
when every night the sky was pink with arson.
He ran a bar beneath the el, the Blarney Stone,
and there one Easter day he sat us down
and made us tape as much as he could play;
'I gave you these. Make sure you put that down',
meaning all he didn't have to say.

All that summer we slept on fire escapes,
or tried to sleep, while sirens or the brass
from our neighbour's Tito Puente tapes
kept us up and made us late for Mass.
I found our back door bent back to admit
beneath the thick sweet reek of grass
a nest of needles, bottle caps, and shit.
By August Tom had sold the Blarney Stone
to Puerto Ricans, paid his debts in cash
but left enough to fly his body home.

The bar still rises from the South Bronx ash,
its yellow neon buzzing in the noonday
dark beneath the el, a sheet-steel door
bolted where he played each second Sunday.
'Play me one I've never heard before'
I'd say, and whether he recalled those notes
or made them up, or – since it was Tom who played –
whether it was something in his blood
(cancer, and he was childless and afraid)
I couldn't tell you. And he always would.

A Reprieve

'Realizing that few of the many tunes remembered from boyhood days
. . . were known to the galaxy of Irish musicians domiciled in Chicago,
the writer decided to have them preserved in musical notation. This was
the initial step in a congenial work which has filled in the interludes of a
busy and eventful life.'
          – Police Chief Francis O'Neil, *Irish Folk Music: A Fascinating Hobby,
          with some Account of Related Subjects* (Chicago 1910)

Here in Chicago it's almost dawn
and quiet in the cell in Deering Street stationhouse
apart from the first birds at the window and the milkwagon
and the soft slap of the club in Chief O'Neil's palm.
'Think it over,' he says, 'but don't take all day.'
Nolan's hands are brown with a Chinaman's blood.
But if he agrees to play three jigs
slowly, so O'Neil can take them down,
he can walk home, change clothes,
and disappear past the stockyards and across the tracks.

Indiana is waiting. O'Neil lowers his eyes,
knowing the Chinaman's face will heal, the Great Lakes
roll in their cold grey sheets and wake,
picket lines will be charged, girls raped
in the sweatshops, the clapboard tenements burn.
And he knows that Nolan will be gone by then,
the coppery stains wiped from the keys of the blackwood flute.

Five thousand miles away Connaught sleeps.
The coast lights dwindle out along the west.
But there's music here in this lamplit cell,
and O'Neil scratching in his manuscript like a monk
at his illuminations, and Nolan's sweet tone breaking
as he tries to phrase a jig the same way twice:
'The Limerick Rake' or 'Tell her I am' or 'My Darling Asleep'.

Theodora, Theodora

Tomorrow, Parnassus. Tonight, outside the taverna,
you wait in the darkened coach alone
flaking *kif* into a roll-up by the dashboard light.
Plates crash. The band risk a verse or two
of a song they played before the war in brothels
where you fucked, gambled, and somehow failed
to die; a song about a girl who didn't.
For love. Slum music. Knives and despair.
Softly you sing what words you can remember.

There are stars in the chorus, and two brothers,
hashish, wisteria, a straight razor. You can't recall
the name of the song or the name of the girl
who bleeds to death at dawn by birdsong before the basilica,
but they're the same. It's been so long.
The bishops banned it, and the colonels,
and somehow even you – how else could you forget –
because these songs have backstreets much like this.
Bile and retsina. Streets the cops don't like.

Sixteen bars then into *Zorba*. The tour-group clap,
snap pictures, then stumble on board laughing
in accents of Buenos Aires or Chicago,
where coach drivers wait outside bars on the south side,
singing softly, for no one but themselves tonight,
of girls who bleed for love. 'Theodora.'
You remember. 'Theodora.' Singing too loud,
you take the slow road back to the hotel.

Down

The stars are shuffling slowly round
Burning in the dark
Upon the lips of angry men
Drinking in the park.
Five thousand fed. I read it in
The Gospel of St Mark.

Helicopters insect round
Above the burned-out cars.
Here where Gospel testified
Between the wars
His harp of darkness cried and prayed
To bottleneck guitars.

Tell me why's you cryin' baby?
I sure would like to know.
Tell me why's you cryin' baby?
I sure would like to know.
Some words I can't make out, and then,
I'll come walkin' through that door.

These flattened thirds and sevenths
Justified the Blues:
Intervals ruled by celestial laws,
Horse, and booze.
Woke up this morning's just the kind
Of line he couldn't use.

Cicadas carve across this night
Their lapidary phrase,
And the darkness children fear
They continually praise.
The darkness children fear, they
Continually praise.

The Classics

I remember it like it was last night,
Chicago, the back room of Flanagan's
malignant with accordions and cigarettes,
Joe Cooley bent above his Paolo Soprani,
its asthmatic bellows pumping as if to revive
the half-corpse strapped about it.
It's five a.m. Everyone's packed up.
His brother Seamus grabs Joe's elbow mid-arpeggio.
'Wake up, man. We have to catch a train.'
His eyelids fluttering, opening. The astonishment . . .

I saw this happen. Or heard it told so well
I've staged the whole drunk memory:
What does it matter now? It's ancient history.
Who can name them? Where lie their bones and armour?

III. True

The Chamber of Errors

It never gets as crowded as Tussaud's,
But every day we draw the curious few
Who've seen our sticker on the underground,
Our card in a phone box, and felt
That, somehow, it was printed just for them.
Of course, it was. Step in and look around.
You haven't come for Marilyn or Elvis.
Like you, I loathe that taxidermal bathos.
We use the faces left in photobooths
By rushed commuters. Their eyes already closed,
We only have to make them *look* like wax.

Now look you on the unfamiliar dead.
More than the pancaked meat in satin caskets,
More than the unforgiving memories,
These are your unforgiven. But be warned,
Like faces glimpsed in fever on the curtains,
These will never truly go away.
Look round, and after, should you need to rest,
And many do, there is a chesterfield.
But please, please, this is important,

Don't touch. I spend my life repairing details.
See where I've pressed the hairs in one by one?
And here? See where I've whorled the fingerpads?
I can't think what possesses people. *Christ*,
Sometimes, at night, I find the faces gouged.

Reliquary

The robot camera enters the *Titanic*
And we see her fish-cold nurseries on the news;
The toys of Pompeii trampled in the panic;
The death camp barrel of babyshoes;

The snow that covered up the lost girl's tracks;
The scapular she wore about her neck;
The broken doll the photojournalist packs
To toss into the foreground of the wreck.

Ovation

O pilgrim from above led through these flames,
There was a time I looked down on a thousand torches.

My voice brought such an echo of applause
You'd think each word a stone dropped in a well.

Our Land. Splash. *Justice long denied.*
Splash. *The humble exalted,*

The exalted . . . and so forth. Immortal words.
It was like love. And my queen loved me,
Could quote my book verbatim.

Then that winter underground, and the golden dream
Defiled by weaklings whispering like burning fat.
Even she was heard to whisper, my Isolde.

I hanged the astrologer, and slipped beneath my tongue
The key to the drawer in which lay locked
The cyanide, the Luger, and my speeches . . .

She would ridicule me in the end,
Quoting them to me verbatim.

Co-Pilot

He leadeth me in the paths of righteousness,
Sitting on my shoulder like a pirate's parrot,
Whispering the Decalogue like a tiny Charlton Heston.
Tch, he goes. *Tch Tch*. He boreth me spitless.

Tonight I need a party with a bottomless punchbowl
Brimming cool vodka to the lip of the horizon.
I'll yank him from his perch and hold him under
Until the bubbles stop.

Cage,

The composer, locked in a soundproof room in Harvard
Heard his heartbeat and the sound of Niagara Falls
Produced by the operation of his nervous system,
From which he derived a theory, no doubt.

Me, I heard a throaty click at the end of 'wedlock'.
And Niagara on the long-distance line.
I knew a couple once, went up there on their honeymoon.
After a week, they said, you don't even hear it.

Meridian

There arc two kinds of people in the world.
Roughly. First there are the kind who say
'There are two kinds of people in the world'
And then there's those who don't.

Me, I live smack on the borderline,
Where the road ends with towers and searchlights,
And we're kept awake all night by the creak of the barrier
Rising and falling like Occam's razor.

Lives of the Artists

I. The Age of Criticism

The clergy, who are prone to vertigo,
Dictate to heaven with a megaphone.
And those addressing Michelangelo
As he was freeing David from the stone
As much as said they thought the nose too big.
He waited till he got them on their own,
Scooped some marble dust up with his tools,
And climbing loftily atop his rig,
He tapped his chisel for those squinting fools
And let a little dust fall on their faces.

He tapped and tapped. And nothing slowly changed
Except for the opinions of Their Graces.

II. The Discovery and Loss of Perspective

Her personal vanishing point,
she said, came when she leant
against his study door
all warm and wet and whispered
'Paolo. Bed.'

He only muttered,
gazing down his grid, 'Oh,
what a lovely thing perspective is!'
She went to live
with cousins in Madrid.

III. *The Advance of Naturalism*

As any dripping clepsydra, batsqueak
In the eaves, or square of angry birds,
So Donatello's steady chisel rhythm
Could sound like words. Perhaps you've read
How someone put his ear against a crack
And heard him try to make a statue speak.
Well, I was there. I heard it answer back.

Of all the cheek! it said, *Show some respect!*
The hand that makes us perfect makes us each
Submissive to the other's intellect.
Nor have we any confidence to teach
Through speaking sculpture or through sculptured speech.

Signifyin' Monkey

'Never write a check with your mouth your ass can't cash.'
– Zach Newton

O.K. I'll tell it, but only if you buy lunch.
One summer I worked nights for Vigil-Guard,
the Chicago security firm. The work was easy:
sitting. And close to home. Ten minutes on the train.
And every night I passed the same fluorescent sign
somewhere in Chinatown: FIGHTER MONKEY.

I paid it no mind. It was the year of the monkey.
I thought I'd try it out one day for lunch.
Risky, I figured, but it's always a good sign
if the sign's in English. I wasn't made chief guard
for nothing, you know. It takes a week to train
on half pay so don't think it's all that easy.
Security's an art. I just make it *look* easy,
like the day I walked home past Fighter Monkey.
Looking back, I wish I'd caught that train,
but I was after a cheap pork feng shui lunch.
Something out front put me on my guard,
though, something about that Day-Glo sign,
the smell, and the cages in the windows, and no sign
of a menu anywhere, which made me a little uneasy,
when out steps this white guy built like a bodyguard
wearing a T-shirt showing a shrieking monkey.
He just stands there, chin out. 'Still serving lunch?'
I ask. 'This is no restaurant,' he says. 'I train
animals' – He's got this tight whisper – 'I train
Barbary Apes using American Sign
Language.' O.K. I figure he's out to lunch,
a potential situation. 'Take it easy,'
I tell him. 'I made a mistake. *You* train monkeys . . .
I represent a firm called Vigil-Guard.'
Turns out he once trained dogs for Vigil-Guard.
And he pays me there and then to help him train

93

one of his babies, a kind of Rottweiler monkey
that took her orders and talked back in Sign.
I swear she must have weighed forty pounds easy.
And teeth! She could have had me for lunch.
Shit, she could have had me *and* lunch!
Then he hauls out this heavy, padded armguard.
'Put that on,' he says. 'This part is safe and easy.
She's going to come at you like a freight train.
Freeze.' I remember he laughed as he made the sign.
The asshole. Lost a thumb to his own monkey.

It's easy. Look, he'd been her only trainer.
Guard or no guard, he'd signed 'I'm lunch.'
The blood! Of course they had to shoot the monkey.

Shooting *The Crane People*

It was a hard year and it was always raining.
The first six months they ran at our approach.
But finally, by patience and cunning,
we gained their trust. Or they learned to ignore us.

Their dialect is noisy and almost unlearnable.
There are no vowels. Their name for themselves,
for example, is a hiss followed by a tiny choking sound
and means 'we', but homophones abound.

Their name for us, a sharp intake of breath,
is also the word for mudslides, or a large, inedible carcass.
We found pronunciation difficult and the slightest error
was met with confusion, irritation, and contempt.

Though excellent telegenic material,
they couldn't recognize themselves on screen.
They move like cranes, and when they squat to dig for grubs
it's like the start of a sad slow dance.

They found our camera terrifying
and were eager to learn to use it.
Our guide would video his wives to punish them.
It was a hard year. I didn't like them. It was always raining.

Banzai

'Don't be nervous. Be hungry.'
Donovan refilled my *sake*.

The chairman was taller than I expected.
He sat at the head of the table,
Donovan between us to translate.

Looking at Donovan, he spoke to me
of risks, profits and futures, and
when Donovan crossed his fingers and winked,
I made my move, surprising myself.
'Tell him I want a taste of power.'
Donovan frowned with the effort.

A chrysanthemum pattern of glassy flesh
arrived which the chairman had ordered for us,
with gravity, several lifetimes earlier –
an expensive, mildly neurotoxic sashimi,
prepared by licensed chefs. Occasionally fatal.
He pincered a morsel, blinked, and swallowed.
Slainte he said, speaking to Donovan, looking at me.

Becoming Catastrophic

Purification itself takes several days. It is agonizing: explosive diarrhoea, sweats, retching, shaking, itching, freezing. But by the second morning the flesh turns white and gradually transparent. Fat, hair, and muscle are the last to go, until finally the tough black dots of the pupils wink out and you see through the world's eyes at last. This is why, having never been corporeal, Thrones, Principalities, Dominions and Powers cannot be depicted except as fortuitous events. Mate in five moves, say. And this is why, once invisible, pains must be taken to think invisibly, for to look too greenly on some sunlit apple's green ebullience can spark a plebiscite, freak hail, sunshower. Remember you are not omnipresent, only infinitely responsible. Always eat alone; your unassimilated food and waste may be visible for hours.

True

n 7 (as of a compass bearing) according to the earth's
geographical rather than magnetic poles. True north.
vb 15 (tr) to adjust so as to make true.

i. A grand magic lantern entertainment

ONE NIGHT ONLY
illustrated by over FORTY DISSOLVENT VIEWS of a strictly moral
character. Nothing to offend the most fastidious person.

Scriptural Views   Comic Songs and Speeches
Lord Franklin setting out to discover a northwest passage
AROUND THE POLE!

The Esquimeaux of the Labradors are aboriginals with no relig-
ious rite. Instead they catch beneath the ice a small, somewhat
poisonous silver fish which they consume uncooked. This practice
induces fever and vivid dreams, and they prognosticate by reading
in the putrified viscera of seals.

Lord Franklin has just read 'Ulysses',
Tennyson's latest, and collapses
his brass collapsible telescope.

> *Twas homeward bound one night on the deep*
> *Swinging in my hammock I fell asleep.*
> *I dreamt a dream and I thought it true*
> *Concerning Franklin and his gallant crew.*

In June, becalmed in sight of a Swedish whaler,
Lord Franklin signalled her captain
to dinner followed by a game of backgammon.
But the long day waned and the sails filled,
and the English waved from the deck
till they were out of sight.
Old age hath yet its honour and its toil.

'One of our visitors held a pocketwatch to his ear. Supposing it to be alive, he asked if it was good to eat. Another, handed a wineglass, appeared very much astonished that it did not melt in the heat of his hand as he entertained a notion that it was made of ice.'

ii. Franklin missing

With a hundred seamen he sailed away
On the frozen ocean in the month of May.
In Baffin Bay where the whale fish below
The fate of Franklin no man may know.

'With interest which accumulates by the hour do we watch for
the return of these two vessels which are perhaps even now
working their way through the Bering Strait into the Pacific.'

The Sikh boy dims
a fringed gas lamp.
Mme Murphy, the sensitive,
bids Lady Franklin sit.

'Please join hands and empty your minds
of all worldly thoughts.'
She summons the spirit
of Sir John Franklin.

Silence in the perfumed dark.
The carriage clock needs winding.

Swedenborg, she explains,
holds that angels,
being purely selfless beings,
generate rather than take up space.
Jammed wing to wing, the halls of heaven
are vast and empty as the ice pack.

Someone coughs and fidgets.
'Wait . . . I see . . . I see . . .
No more today. Please. The palpitations.
Fetch the ladies' coats, Mahapatra,
and show Lord Merryll in.'

iii. The search party

And now my burden it gives me pain
To think my Franklin lies across the Main.
Ten thousand pounds would I freely give
To say on earth that my Franklin does live.

'We pressed on and discovered at four o clock
two skeletons in furs face down in the ice.
We scattered black matchstick bones
from one braided sleeve and found they'd clutched
a toothbrush and a silver medal for navigation
awarded by the Royal Naval College, 1830,
and the remains of a letter of which was legible:

"... all spoilt. Seven hundred tins in all. Several strong men
fainted and wee drew lots to put out with ... the long boat to
look for free wather. On the 12th night of our hawl, brother
Dick, wee saw 2 very large hice Burgh to windward of ous and
we stopt in thare shadow for to rest in the boat for the wether
was bad and weed be out of the wind. Apon taking off his boots
wee see Capten Hughs has no payne in his feet and says they feel
warm but wee feer he will soon loose them. We are most blynded
from the hice and I feer, dear friends, I canot rite very longer for
my eyes hurt full sore and I am week for want of food. Tell
mother I die a Chrischun in Gods mercee

                              Good by untell we meet in heven,
                              Tom Cook"

For what we found next I regret I can offer
neither explanation nor conjecture,
for we discovered scattered about beneath half-buried sledges
seventy silk handkerchiefs, five pocket watches,
a badminton racket, a birdcage, a tiny clockwork cricket,
a brass telescope, and several barrel organs,
their gearwork still in fair condition.
One of these last I tested, and winding its handle
I succeeded in producing a medley from popular operettas
until a storm blew up and we struck back for camp.'

Privacy

Here, as in life, they were admitted
to a club exclusive as the Garrick,
now a kind of Victorian Angkor Wat
adjacent to the A road.
Their mossed, sepulchral pieties
neglected for decades, swallowed
back into a mild jungle,
their shapeless sculpture decked
flat, sprayed with uncouth rhymes,
their eminent corpses
violated by ritual necrophilia in the 60s,
how fares it with the happy dead?

The PM urges their revival,
the spirits of industry, exploration,
eels and gin, the floorless jig.
Here, everyone knows his place.
Here, little green bronze bells
festoon the exterior of the 'Egyptian' mausoleum.
The strings once led inside,
where, waking in their two inch dark,
the prematurely interred
could tintinnabulate as if for tea.
Sadly, these have snapped.

The Raindial

The sun goes in. The light goes out.
A million shadows fade away.
It could be any time of day.
Now dream that you don't dream about
The garden of this Hackney squat
Where dark drops stipple on the *Sun*,
The umbrella skeleton,
The sink, the broken flowerpot . . .

A cold rain slicks the garden path
That leads you down the overgrowth
Toward the monument to Thoth:
A drowned shark in a birdbath.

Above its fin the zodiac
Spins upon its sentinel.
The gnomon knows, but will not tell
The time nor give your future back.
The gnomon knows. And round it's writ
As these long   pass swift away
So too the hope of man decays.
TippExed under pigeonshit,
The years, the months, the weeks, the days.

The Brother

Dropping a canapé in my Beaujolais
At some reception, opening or launch,
I recall briefly the brother I never had
Presiding at less worldly rituals:
The only man at my wedding not wearing a tie;
Avuncular, swaddling my nephew over the font;
Thumbing cool oil on our mother's forehead
In the darkened room, the bells and frankincense . . .
While the prodigal sweats in the strip-lit corridor.

Now, picture us facing each other, myself and the brother
I never met: two profiles in silhouette,
Or else a chalice, depending how you look.
Imagine that's this polystyrene cup.
I must break bread with my own flesh and blood.

Fraction

The fourteenth time my mother told the story
Of her cousins dismembered by a British bomb,
I turned on her, her Irish son. 'I'm American.
I was born here.' She went to pieces.

And would not be solaced. I had her eyes,
The aunt's, that is, who, the story goes,
Was brought to the jail to sort the bits in tubs.
Toes. I meant to renounce such grotesque pity.

I was thirteen. I didn't know who I was. She knew.
As I held her wrists, reassuring,
Repeating, that I was her Irish son,
I was the man who'd clicked the toggle switch

Bracing himself between two branches,
Between the flash and the report.

Erratum

I touch the cold flesh of a god in the V and A,
the guard asleep in his chair, and I'm shocked
to find it's plaster. These are the reproduction rooms,
where the David stands side by side with the Moses
and Trajan's column (in two halves).
It reminds me of the inventory sequence in *Citizen Kane*.
It reminds me of an evening twenty years ago.

And all at once I'm there, at her side,
turning the pages as she plays
from the yellowed song sheets I rescued from a bookstall:
Dodd's setting of *Antony and Cleopatra*. All very improving.
'Give me my robe and crown,' she warbles
in a Victorian coloratura. 'I have immoral longings in me.'

I want to correct her – the word on the page is
immortal – but I'm fourteen and scandalized.
(I knew there were no innocent mistakes.
I'd finished *Modern Masters: Freud*
before she snatched and burned it. 'Filth' –
yanking each signature free of the spine,
'Filth. Filth. Filth.')

The song is over. But when she smiles at me,
I'm on the verge of tears, staring down at the gap-
toothed grimace of our old Bechstein. 'What's wrong?'
What's *wrong*? I check the word again. She's right. Immoral.
She shows me the printer's slip, infecting
the back page of every copy, like,
she might have said, the first sin.

The guard snorts in his dream. I take my palm away
still cool from what I'd taken to be marble.
And when I get that moment back, it's later;
I'm sobbing on her shoulder and I can't say why.
So she suggests another visit to the furnace, where,
to comfort me, perhaps, we rake the cinders with the music
till they chink and spark, and shove the pages
straight to the white core to watch them darken as if ageing,
blacken, enfold, like a sped-up film of blossoms in reverse.

Some Notes

The Hunter's Purse – 'Well, they used to come by emigrants coming home on holidays, mostly, because they'd imagine if they posted them they'd be broken, which they would at the time. And it was all returned Americans coming home to see their own native place again that brought both the gramophones and the records. And there was as much lookout for an emigrant returning home that time as there would be for – I don't know what now, to see an aeroplane going into orbit or something off the ground. Because there was an awful lookout for John McKenna's records, an awful lookout.' – Tommy Gilmartin, quoted by Harry Bradshaw and Jackie Small in 'John McKenna, Leitrim's master of the Concert flute' (*Musical Traditions*, No. 7, 1987).

A Repertoire – 'Play me one we've never heard before.' Chicago fiddler Liz Carroll would ask this of the late Johnny McGreevy who would alway comply. But the poem is not about Johnny.

Theodora, Theodora – In 'The Gangster Reformed, A study in musical parallels' Jaoa Dos Santos compares the subcultures of Tango, Fado, and Rembetika (*Musical Traditions*, No. 7, 1987). He might also consider the lifespan of urban Blues.

Down – What I heard of the song was sung by Jimmy Reed.

Lives of the Artists – Three misremembered episodes from Vasari's lives of, respectively, Michelangelo, Uccello, and Donatello. He remarks that the latter used to mutter to his favourite piece, the *Zuccone*, 'Speak, or the plague take you!'

Signifyin' Monkey – is the title of an R&B standard. Vigil-Guard were a private security firm on Chicago's west side. Zach Newton was my supervisor there.

Banzai – *Fugu* (*Canthigaster riulatus*, *Fugu rubripes* or Pacific puffer-fish), if improperly filleted of its liver and roe, causes paralysis and death within minutes.

True – Most of it is. The song is a Victorian broadside I got from the singing of Micheal O'Domhnaill. Some of the other quotations are from Ross, Captain John, *A Voyage of Discovery in HM Ships 'Isabella and*

Alexander' (John Murray, 1819) and Lord Egerton in the *London Quarterly Review* (June 1847), which is quoted in Evan S. Connell's account of the Franklin expedition in *A Long Desire* (Holt Reinhart and Winston, 1977). Other quotations are trued.